for
all
who
wander

JOURNEY GUIDE

for
all
who
wander

Why Knowing
God Is Better
Than Knowing
It All

(in)courage author

robin dance

with **mary carver**

B&H
PUBLISHING
NASHVILLE, TENNESSEE

978-1-5359-7984-9

Published by B&H Publishing Group
Nashville, Tennessee

1 2 3 4 5 6 7 • 24 23 22 21 20

To all the Wanderers
longing to find their way home.

CONTENTS

Sweet Friend,

Would it surprise you to know that I've already prayed for you? My heart is tender toward those who long to believe but who also wrestle with hard and holy things. I'm convinced that as you seek God, you will find Him. His very Word promises us we will, yes, but finding Him has also been my experience despite my own questions and doubts. This Journey Guide is a resource to help you along the way.

At first it may seem like *For All Who Wander* is just a story of me struggling with my faith, but I hope you'll see, more than anything, it is a portrait of God's faithfulness, which means you share in it, too. Sure, I've put a chunk of my story into the pages of a book, but this Journey Guide will help *you* do the same. Different from a Bible study or workbook, it is designed to help you process your own story of faith and to see how your wandering is a way back to God.

My friends at DaySpring, (in)courage, and LifeWay and I are passionate about you knowing God, plain and simple. If you're willing to invest a little time in working through this Journey Guide, you'll come to know God better as you engage His words found in Scripture and align your life to what you discover about Him. As you contemplate where you are spiritually and examine your life, let down your guard and open your heart to God. When you do, you'll be making space for the Holy Spirit to accomplish holy work.

How you use the Journey Guide is entirely up to you, but ideally we'd recommend you join a group of friends and make it a five-week adventure, tackling five chapters at a time. You might find value in adding an extra week at the beginning for members to become better acquainted, to cast vision, and set expectation for the weeks to come. Or you may want to tack on an extra session at the end to discuss how you've grown in your faith over the previous weeks, acknowledging and celebrating God's faithfulness and new revelation of Himself to you.

Each chapter of the Journey Guide is purposefully divided into four sections, as described below:

READ: In this section, you'll find Scripture that correlates to the book chapter you are reading, intended to point you to God while also establishing your mind-set for the sections to follow.

REFLECT: Here, you'll ponder thought-provoking questions to help you consider *your* story and circumstances. As I share my experiences and inner dialogue, these reflection questions will move you beyond my story and into your own, helping you think more deeply about God's "withness" in your life and to become increasingly aware of God's faithfulness. Some questions might bring conviction and a genuine desire to be transformed, but you will always find great encouragement for what God wants to do in your life. These questions will also help create wonderful discussion among your small group! Especially if you're going through five chapters every time you gather, every member will have a lot to draw from in order to contribute to a lively conversation. Don't feel the pressure to answer every question, but do let the questions point you to God.

RESOLVE: This section offers a call to action designed to either impress a spiritual truth, move you to apply something you've learned, challenge your habits and thoughts, or help you better understand how God is working in and through your life. If you determine now to see the value in each exercise, you will get the most out of this Journey Guide. Like most things in life, the more you put into this experience, the more you'll gain. Again, every call to action may not be something that resonates with you, and that is okay! Let the ideas you find be springboards for your own ideas.

PRAY: As each section is ended in prayer, we encourage you to have conversations with God in light of each chapter, where you're free to admit the truth of your heart while inviting God to meet your need and reveal more of Himself to you.

This is heart-work, dear one, but I am confident of this very thing: that He who has begun a good work in you will be faithful to complete it!

With love and great expectation,

robin

THE WAY IN A MANGER

READ

At that time the disciples came to Jesus and asked, "So who is greatest in the kingdom of heaven?" He called a child and had him stand among them. "Truly I tell you," he said, "unless you turn and become like children, you will never enter the kingdom of heaven. Therefore, whoever humbles himself like this child—this one is the greatest in the kingdom of heaven. And whoever welcomes one child like this in my name welcomes me." (Matt. 18:1–5)

REFLECT

Jesus often responded to people in unexpected ways, counter to culture or convention. In this passage in Matthew, He shows regard and love for children—those whom His culture often overlooked, assuming they had nothing of value to offer.

A child's faith, and even that of a new believer, is accepting, eager, and wholehearted. Take a few moments to think about the beginning of your own faith story.

When did you first hear about God? Do you recall your initial impressions about Jesus?

_____

_____

_____

_____

_____

What is your first memory of church?

_____

_____

_____

_____

_____

Who had the greatest influence on your early faith journey?

_____

_____

_____

_____

_____

Can you identify beliefs, habits, or practices from your childhood that you later recognized as untrue, unbiblical, or perhaps merely a "tradition of man"?

_____

_____

_____

_____

_____

How are you a better (or different) person because of your history with the church?

_____

_____

_____

_____

_____

RESOLVE

Let's make sure we appreciate our beginnings, small or large as they may have been. And let's appreciate the people who made them possible.

Write a thank-you note or pick up a meaningful card for the person or people who first took you to church or introduced you to the Christian faith. (Even if that person is no longer alive, make this tangible gesture to express your gratitude to them and to God, perhaps by recording an entry in your journal or writing an acknowledgment somewhere in your Bible.) Be sure to follow through and mail the letter. Or, if you happened to end up at church or coming to faith on your own solely by the leading of the Holy Spirit, write a note of appreciation to the leaders or mentors who have influenced your growth.

PRAY

Father God, You are sovereign, in control of all things and perfect in all Your ways. Thank You for the unique way You have invited me into life with Christ for now and into eternity. I'm so glad for the gift of memories, how we can look back over our lives and see Your hand at work. I'm grateful for every leader, teacher, family member, and friend who has pointed me to You, and I ask Your blessing and favor over their lives now. Help me to identify things I've learned through the years that simply aren't true or biblical; ideas, doctrine, or principles tangled up in man-made traditions. Help me love others with reckless abandon, the way You love me, and move me forward in this journey that can seem so foggy at times. Thank You for Jesus—that He loved me enough to die for me and walk with me through the ups and downs of this life. Amen.

2

LOST AT THE COUNTY FAIR

READ

"Haven't I commanded you: be strong and courageous? Do not be afraid or discouraged, for the LORD your God is with you wherever you go." (Josh. 1:9)

Where can I go to escape your Spirit? Where can I flee from your presence? (Ps. 139:7)

"And remember, I am with you always, to the end of the age." (Matt. 28:20)

Be satisfied with what you have, for he himself has said, "I will never leave you or abandon you." (Heb. 13:5b)

REFLECT

As the verses above remind us, it is so helpful to know that God isn't just *for* us, He is always *with* us. In this chapter I've shared a few instances of when I was lost or at least felt that way, and it led me to consider how many different ways a person might be lost. More importantly, I see these moments as varied ways God can meet us right where we are. I wonder if it might be interesting for you to think about as well.

9

Have you ever been lost? What was your first reaction? How did you find your
way back to safety/the known?

_____

_____

_____

_____

_____

If not currently, can you recall a time you felt spiritually lost? If so, what was your
response? Did you immediately seek out help, or did you remain isolated? How
might you fight against the urge to remain alone when you're feeling discon-
nected spiritually?

_____

_____

_____

_____

_____

In what ways has God met you in the lost places, proving He's actually with you
even though it doesn't feel like it? What things, experiences, circumstances, or
people did He use to help you see Him just a little bit more in the dark moments?

_____

_____

_____

_____

_____

RESOLVE

Sometimes creating something tangible can help us organize our thoughts, reveal something we previously missed, or commit new ideas to memory. So, let's get creative as we process our walk with God. Draw a time line of your life, being sure to include milestone events and significant experiences. Include objective facts such as dates and places, as well as more emotional markers such as how each experience made you feel or influenced your faith. I think you will be enlightened and possibly surprised by what you see. Include times God showed up for you because these are the moments that help us look back and realize He was always with us. They increase our faith to believe He is here even now.

PRAY

Father God, thank You for the reminders in Your Word that You are not only *for* me, You are *with* me. It is almost overwhelming to know that You rejoice over me with gladness and delight over me with singing. When I find myself "within a dark wood where the straight way was lost,"[1] remind me that You are a warrior who saves. At my lowest moments, when I'm tempted to be fearful, help me to believe the things You say about me—that I am Your child, that no one and no thing can snatch me out of Your hand, and even if I feel alone I am not, because You never abandon me. I am so thankful You are big enough to handle my questions and doubts, and I'm amazed how You can use these things to draw me closer to You. I praise You for the mysterious ways You redeem my wandering with purpose. To You be the glory forever and ever. Amen.

3

WHISKER RUBS AND PEOPLE-PLEASERS

READ

For am I now trying to persuade people, or God? Or am I striving to please people? If I were still trying to please people, I would not be a servant of Christ. (Gal. 1:10)

. . . just as we have been approved by God to be entrusted with the gospel, so we speak, not to please people, but rather God, who examines our hearts. (1 Thess. 2:4)

REFLECT

Are you a people-pleaser? Write down some environments in which you are more concerned with pleasing the people around you rather than God.

_____

_____

_____

_____

_____

Would you consider yourself a peacemaker or a peacekeeper? Can you point to a victory when you "made" peace (engaged conflict) rather than just "kept" peace (avoided conflict)?

_____

_____

_____

_____

_____

What are the influences that contributed to these tendencies in your life?

_____

_____

_____

_____

_____

Do your actions consistently align with what you profess about your faith?

_____

_____

_____

_____

_____

RESOLVE

Find a rough, unfinished piece of wood that has at least one flat surface, and smooth it with a coarse grade of sandpaper. Using paints or a marker, write out Galatians 1:10, and place your finished artwork somewhere you'll be reminded of your desire to please an audience of one. Then, take a moment to invite God to show you where you've fallen into performance, where you may be seeking the approval of man in place of pleasing Him, and any areas in your life where you're keeping peace instead of making peace. Ask the Lord to transform your heart to care most about pleasing Him.

PRAY

Father God, I know too often I'm concerned about the approval of other people, but I want to be concerned most about pleasing You. Please forgive me when I get that backwards. Help me to find confidence in pursuing true peace and to becoming increasingly dissatisfied with anything less. Reveal to me any habits or practices in my life that cause me to look to others to fill a void when it's You I need more than anything. I know that Your Word says that those who are in the flesh cannot please God, which makes me even more thankful for Your Spirit who lives in me to fight sin and remind me that I am your daughter (Rom. 8:8–9). Amen.

4

TESTIMONY ENVY

READ

Blessed is the God and Father of our Lord Jesus Christ, who has blessed us with every spiritual blessing in the heavens in Christ. For he chose us in him, before the foundation of the world, to be holy and blameless in love before him. He predestined us to be adopted as sons through Jesus Christ for himself, according to the good pleasure of his will, to the praise of his glorious grace that he lavished on us in the Beloved One.

In him we have redemption through his blood, the forgiveness of our trespasses, according to the riches of his grace that he richly poured out on us with all wisdom and understanding. He made known to us the mystery of his will, according to his good pleasure that he purposed in Christ as a plan for the right time—to bring everything together in Christ, both things in heaven and things on earth in him.

In him we have also received an inheritance, because we were predestined according to the plan of the one who works out everything in agreement with the purpose of his will, so that we who had already put our hope in Christ might bring praise to his glory.

In him you also were sealed with the promised Holy Spirit when you heard the word of truth, the gospel of your salvation, and when you believed (Eph. 1:3–13).

REFLECT

When it comes to where a person stands with God, some believers "know that they know that they know"—meaning they never waver in their assurance of salvation, maybe because theirs was a dramatic conversion to faith. But even if we came to faith in a much more subtle way, God provides assurances throughout Scripture about the permanence of our standing with Him, just like in this rich passage in Ephesians. As I learned, a testimony doesn't have to be dramatic to be real. A testimony is simply the story of Jesus working in your life, whether when He first introduced Himself to you or what He is doing in your life today. Think about your own story:

When did you first recognize your need for a Savior, confess your sin and ask for forgiveness, turn in repentance, and receive Christ?

_____

_____

_____

_____

_____

Was yours a Damascus Road experience, or a quieter road to faith? Do you ever wish you had a more exciting (or less exciting) story? Explain.

_____

_____

_____

_____

_____

Have you shared your salvation story with others or told someone how you see Jesus moving in your life right now?

_____

_____

_____

_____

_____

Did you notice in this chapter how Paul was wandering from God on the way to *kill* the church, while I was wandering in the midst of *serving* the church? Wandering can look different for each one of us. What does it look like in your life?

_____

_____

_____

_____

_____

RESOLVE

If you have never shared your salvation story, consider sharing it with a friend. It doesn't have to be a formal presentation; it could simply start with, "Have I ever told you about how (or why or when) I became a Christian?" Or you could make it a bit more casual and say, "Have I ever told you why I go to church?" Or if it's more relevant, reach out to someone who needs to hear how God is working in your life right now.

If sharing your testimony feels too intimidating, first try writing it down. Type or write it in your own handwriting; then laminate it, scrapbook it, or slip it in your Bible. This is one story that will be a treasure in the years to come for you and your family.

PRAY

Father God, thank You for the way You're writing my story, for pursuing me and saving me from the penalty of my sin according to Your perfect will and in your equally perfect timing. Help me to believe the things you say about me, and to trust Your ways when it's tempting to question You. Thank You that my salvation story is written exactly how You wanted it to be written. Moving from death to life is a miracle no matter how it looks, and I'm grateful. Please forgive me when I fail to see the plan You've imagined for my life, when I wander away from Your truth and I'm tempted to want anything else. Give me the courage to be bold in my faith, to share with others the hope I've found in Christ, eager even, to explain the difference You've made in my life. Oh, how I love You. Help me to love You more. For Your glory always. Amen.

5

A SAME KIND OF DIFFERENT

READ

"I am the true vine, and my Father is the gardener. Every branch in me that does not produce fruit he removes, and he prunes every branch that produces fruit so that it will produce more fruit. You are already clean because of the word I have spoken to you. Remain in me, and I in you. Just as a branch is unable to produce fruit by itself unless it remains on the vine, neither can you unless you remain in me. I am the vine; you are the branches. The one who remains in me and I in him produces much fruit, because you can do nothing without me. . . . As the Father has loved me, I have also loved you. Remain in my love." (John 15:1–5, 9)

"I give you a new command: Love one another. Just as I have loved you, you are also to love one another. By this everyone will know that you are my disciples, if you love one another." (John 13:34–35)

REFLECT

In this chapter, Cassie's and Tad's lives revealed an intimate relationship with God as evidenced by how they treated and loved others. Expecting your faith to mature without pursuing intimacy with Christ is cart-before-the-horse living. Their faith wasn't maturing as a result of producing more fruit; fruit was simply a by-product of deepening faith. Has your faith been characterized by striving to produce fruit or performing to impress others at the expense of real relationship with Jesus? Explain.

_____

_____

_____

_____

_____

Who are the people in your life who are "a same kind of different" as Cassie and Tad? How are they unlike other Christians you know, and what is it about them that points you toward Jesus?

_____

_____

_____

_____

_____

In true transformation, outer behavior is merely the expression of an inner change. It is so easy to get wrapped up in producing fruit that we forget about what needs to take place at the root level. Remember, it is strong roots that establish a secure foundation for future health and subsequent growth, and in the life of faith, strong roots develop by abiding in Christ. What steps might you take to abide in Jesus and His love and faithfulness, trusting *Him* to bear fruit rather than trusting in your own ability to work harder?

RESOLVE

A fun, tangible way to remember our need to abide in Christ is to plant an herb garden. Regardless of the weather outside, a quick online search or trip to your local garden center will help you find a way to grow a few of your favorites indoors. As you tend your windowsill or countertop garden, celebrate its growth. Think about what is required for growth to produce healthy stems, leaves, and flowers. Usually this requires soil preparation, then watering and fertilizing according to guidelines, and then exposing the plant to sunlight. As you watch your little herbs grow and consider the requirements for its growth, ponder how that correlates to remaining in Christ, how He is the vine and you are the branches. How *He* can tend to the soil of your heart and be the light and water you need to grow up strong and healthy. Look at your herbs as a living metaphor for deep and abiding faith. And if you aren't blessed with "green thumbs," pick up some fresh rosemary or basil at the grocery store, rub their leaves between your fingers, and then inhale the scent that's left behind. Imagine inhaling the aroma of Christ and inviting Him to change you on the inside.

PRAY

Father God, thank You for the godly people You've placed in my life to show me a glimpse of Jesus. Thank You for how their examples demonstrate the difference in a faith that aligns our hearts with our actions. Help me to trust You to accomplish Your will and Your ways, rather than me striving to do more to earn Your favor or to change from the outside in. Teach me what it means to remain and abide in You, to take You at your word, and for our relationship to grow more deeply. Help me always to be eager to share the difference You've made in my life, and for love, joy, peace, patience, kindness, goodness, gentleness, faithfulness, and self-discipline to abound. Thank You for being the light and water I need to grow. Amen.

6

YOU DON'T KNOW WHAT
YOU DON'T KNOW

READ

But whatever were gains to me I now consider loss for the sake of
Christ. What is more, I consider everything a loss because of the
surpassing worth of knowing Christ Jesus my Lord, for whose sake I
have lost all things. I consider them garbage, that I may gain Christ
and be found in him, not having a righteousness of my own that
comes from the law, but that which is through faith in Christ—the
righteousness that comes from God on the basis of faith. I want
to know Christ—yes, to know the power of his resurrection and
participation in his sufferings, becoming like him in his death. . . .
(Phil. 3:7–10 NIV)

REFLECT

More than anything else in this life and even more so in light of eternity,
knowing God is our greatest treasure. But thinking back to the examples in this
chapter, can you relate to not knowing something you felt like you should have
known, and consequently feeling stupid about it? Or, if you were in a position

where you could feign comprehension, did you come clean or pretend to understand? Did you even know what you didn't know?

When it comes to your faith, do you ever feel like you're "all good" and know everything you need to know? How might your actions suggest this even if you don't actually think you know it all?

_____

_____

_____

_____

_____

Are you active or passive in strengthening your relationship with God? Give examples.

_____

_____

_____

_____

_____

What are some evidences or examples of the Spirit's inner work in your life?

_____

_____

_____

_____

_____

RESOLVE

If you aren't already, commit to being a life-long learner starting *now*. Let's challenge ourselves in two ways:

1. Rather than wringing your hands or feeling ashamed over what you don't know intellectually, biblically, academically, or skill-wise, take a proactive approach. Write down three things you'd like to learn more about in the next year—for instance, a language or a time in history, a people group or religious system, a skill or a technique. *Anything* new will help you feel more confident than you did before. While you can't always know what you don't know, you *can* continue your education and expand your understanding of your faith and your world.

2. Select three passages of Scripture to memorize over the next three months. Choose verses that are meaningful to you and relate specifically to an area in which you long to see change (i.e., if you want to focus on knowing God, you could choose Philippians 3:7–8b and so on). As you hide God's life-giving words in your heart, pray them, too. Invite the Spirit to do the inner work of changing you to conform to the image of Christ by knowing God more intimately.

PRAY

Father, I'm astonished at the depth of Your riches, and that there is always something new I can learn about You. Yes, I know You, but I long to know You even more deeply. Strengthen my confidence and trust in You. Bring conviction where it's needed and diminish the voices that try to defeat me with shame and condemnation. Help me remember that my struggle isn't against flesh and blood but in the spiritual realm, and that You've given me both defensive and offensive armor to protect myself and fight. Give me a teachable and humble heart to grow in my knowledge and understanding of You. I love You, Lord, help me to love You more. Amen.

7

HAMSTER WHEELS

READ

He has shown you, O man, what is good;
And what does the LORD require of you
But to act justly,
To love mercy,
And to walk humbly with your God? (Micah 6:8 NKJV)

"Teacher, which command in the law is the greatest?" [Jesus] said to him, "Love the Lord your God with all your heart, with all your soul, and with all your mind. This is the greatest and most important command. The second is like it: Love your neighbor as yourself." (Matt. 22:36–39)

REFLECT

Have you ever said yes to a church activity or opportunity for service because of a sense of responsibility or obligation? If so, imagine for a moment how things might have been different if you said no.

_____

_____

_____

_____

_____

Are your "yeses" typically driven by your love for God, your desire to please Him, and your longing to know Him and make Him known? Or is guilt informing your choices? If you sifted your decisions through the sieve of Scripture—for instance, the Micah and Matthew passages noted here—would you respond in the same way?

_____

_____

_____

_____

_____

RESOLVE

Make a list of all the ways you're serving the Lord right now. For each item or task, ask yourself why you're doing it. Will it lead you into deeper relationship with God as you seek to bring glory to Him, or will it cause you to take your eyes off Christ and potentially cause you to wander? Are you finding yourself on a hamster wheel, doing Christian-y things out of a sense of obligation or because you're trying to meet expectations of others? Answer honestly and then decide if the answers make a difference in your future choices. If you're recognizing your choices aren't aligning with what the Lord wants for your life, don't assume a false guilt; seize the opportunity to transform your mind (your inner self) so decisions going forward are His best plan for you and the body of Christ. Let go of the items on your list He isn't actually calling you to, and move forward with even more passion in the places He truly is.

PRAY

Father God, thank You for the truth we find in Scripture and for freeing us from trying to reach some unattainable mark of perfection. Thank You, too, that verse after verse, and chapter after chapter, we can learn more about You, and who we are called to be as Your children in light of our relationship. Help me to follow Jesus as I look for ways to glorify You in my service to others. Fill me with Your supernatural grace and strength to accomplish the good things You've called me to, and give me the discernment, resolve, and confidence to say no when I'm serving out of guilt, obligation, or performance. Amen.

8

MOUNTAINS AND VALLEYS

READ

Consider it a great joy, my brothers and sisters, whenever you experience various trials, because you know that the testing of your faith produces endurance. And let endurance have its full effect, so that you may be mature and complete, lacking nothing. (James 1:2–4)

REFLECT

Spend a little time thinking about your past—the last year or even decades back.

Did you face any mountains as they were described in this chapter, obstacles that interfered with your life? What about valleys? Do you recall any dark, lonely, or depressed seasons?

_____

_____

_____

_____

Did you ever wonder if the mountain actually had two sides or if the valley would come to an end? Did you remain isolated or reach out to others for help or encouragement? Put your thoughts to paper to help process.

_____

_____

_____

_____

_____

How did God show up when you were going through a difficult season? Did you sense His presence when you were in the midst of your journey, or was His presence obvious only after you were on the other side?

_____

_____

_____

_____

_____

RESOLVE

Go outside and get some fresh air. Whether you're pounding pavement in your suburban neighborhood or hiking a trail in a nearby park, notice where it might be easy to wander off the beaten path. Pay attention to the elevation, inclines and declines; observe how your muscles and lungs react to various terrains. As you walk uphill, praise God for remaining faithful no matter what obstacles or challenges you face in life. As you walk downhill, thank Him for pursuing you when you sink to emotional valleys and need Him more than ever. You might want to incorporate this practice if you walk or run often for pleasure or health; you will find a closeness with God as you "pray without ceasing."

PRAY

Father God, thank You for Your unchanging nature, that You remain the same yesterday, today, and forever. Give me a heart that praises You no matter what, that I might face the mountains and valleys of life with equal regard, a chance to see and seek You in the midst of rugged terrain. Thank You for redemption in my story—that I'm equipped to understand the trials and tragedies of others because I've lived my unique version of the very same thing. Help me to receive the good and hard experiences of life with the same measure of joy, made possible because my joy is found in You, not in my circumstances. I trust that You are always good, even when I don't understand. You are my greatest treasure. Amen.

9

OPPORTUNITY LOST

READ

For I am not ashamed of the gospel, because it is the power of God for salvation to everyone who believes, first to the Jew, and also to the Greek. For in it the righteousness of God is revealed from faith to faith, just as it is written: The righteous will live by faith. (Rom. 1:16–17)

If then there is any encouragement in Christ, if any consolation of love, if any fellowship with the Spirit, if any affection and mercy, make my joy complete by thinking the same way, having the same love, united in spirit, intent on one purpose. Do nothing out of selfish ambition or conceit, but in humility consider others as more important than yourselves. Everyone should look out not only for his own interests, but also for the interests of others. (Phil. 2:1–4)

REFLECT

Think through the opportunities God has given you over the years.

Have you ever missed an opportunity to share your faith with someone? What held you back? Fear of rejection, being asked a question you aren't able to answer, that you'd be viewed as a Jesus-freak, or something else entirely? Would you say or do anything differently today?

_____

_____

_____

_____

_____

What about the times you *have* shared your faith? Contrast how you felt between sharing and not sharing.

_____

_____

_____

_____

_____

Have you ever considered how sharing the gospel or your testimony *is* a means of looking out for the interests of others as Philippians 2:4 commands?

_____

_____

_____

Can you think of a time when you may have had Christian liberty to do something, but it caused someone else to stumble? Did you try to justify your actions? Did you sense conviction by the Holy Spirit? Explain.

_____

_____

_____

_____

_____

What are some practical ways you can "consider others as more important than yourself"?

_____

_____

_____

_____

_____

RESOLVE

If you're one for whom sharing your faith comes naturally, initiate a conversation about evangelism with a believing friend you know is more reserved. Mentor her by offering practical suggestions or ideas for how she can share her faith with others. But, if you've lived long enough and especially if you've followed Jesus for a while, odds are good that you've missed an opportunity to share your faith with someone who is no longer part of your life. Are you carrying any guilt from not doing so? God isn't condemning you, friend, so here's a simple exercise to remind you of God's goodness:

Find a dry erase board and marker, and write that person's name on it. (If you can think of more than one person, write all the names.) There it is, in writing, out in the open. Confess your conviction to the Lord, acknowledge the forgiveness He's already given to you, and ask Him to give you the boldness to share about your faith in the future. Now—here's the best part—erase the board. Wipe it completely clean and remember that is exactly what Jesus has done in your life, imparting His righteousness to you and washing all your sins as white as snow. Remember, not sharing your faith isn't necessarily a sin. But if you felt a personal conviction, praise our God that He's a patient God, and the God of second chances.

PRAY

Father, I am not ashamed of the gospel! Will You give me the courage and boldness to live what I profess? I'm grateful for the people You send into my life to share about Your grace, love, forgiveness, and redemption. Help me to remember the privilege of carrying the good news to those who need to hear, and to consider those around me more highly than myself. Amen.

10

PATTERNS AND PRACTICE

READ

For we are God's masterpiece. He has created us anew in Christ Jesus, so we can do the good things he planned for us long ago. (Eph. 2:10 NLT)

The one who says he remains in him should walk just as he walked. (1 John 2:6)

REFLECT

Think about your personality as a child, as a younger adult, and now.

Do you see more similarities or differences from your personality today? Is your temperament the same, or have you changed greatly?

_____

_____

_____

_____

_____

Note any evidences of spiritual maturity in your life from work God has done in your heart. Jot down an example of how you have been transformed by the renewing of your mind.

_____

_____

_____

_____

_____

What characteristics of your current disposition would you like to see nurtured as you grow older? Which ones would you like to see diminished or even left behind?

_____

_____

_____

_____

_____

Where do your eyes naturally wander when they aren't on God? To other people, worldly pursuits, or material gain? How can you shift your eyes back to Christ?

_____

_____

_____

_____

_____

What kind of "patterns and practices" can you create right now to grow more like Jesus?

_____

_____

_____

_____

In what ways do you recognize your immeasurable value to God, your own uniqueness, and the "good things" He planned for your life? How can you remind yourself when you forget this?

_____

_____

_____

_____

RESOLVE

If you enjoy personality tests, you probably know your Meyers-Briggs type or Enneagram number off the top of your head. Perhaps you're more interested in strengths or spiritual gifts. If we become more of who we already are (who God created us to be) in our final years, perhaps our personality type could guide us.

Take a handful of descriptions for your personality type (e.g., extroverted, perfectionist, motivating, organized, spontaneous), and think about how you'd like to see those characteristics play out in the future. Now, with your temperament in mind, take a handful of descriptions about Jesus' character, and think about what you'd like to grow in, to become more like Him. How can you change the patterns of your thoughts and practices to become more like Him?

PRAY

Father God, I praise You for the way You've created me, completely unique and bearing Your image. Help me to recognize and appreciate the ways I'm different from others, and the ways others are different from me. Give me the wisdom to use the incredible gifts You've given me as they're intended—to bless those around me and to transform me from the inside out. Guard my mind, my eyes, and my heart from wandering or from falling under the influence of others or our world. More than anything, help me to be ever mindful that my goal is to become more and more like Christ. Amen.

11

BEHIND THE CURTAIN

READ

Older men are to be self-controlled, worthy of respect, sensible, and sound in faith, love, and endurance. In the same way, older women are to be reverent in behavior, not slanderers, not slaves to excessive drinking. *They are to teach what is good, so that they may encourage the young women.* . . . (Titus 2:2–4a, emphasis added)

"Do not judge, so that you won't be judged. For you will be judged by the same standard with which you judge others, and you will be measured by the same measure you use. Why do you look at the splinter in your brother's eye but don't notice the beam of wood in your own eye? Or how can you say to your brother, 'Let me take the splinter out of your eye,' and look, there's a beam of wood in your own eye? Hypocrite! First take the beam of wood out of your eye, and then you will see clearly to take the splinter out of your brother's eye." (Matt. 7:1–5)

REFLECT

Like the friend I mentioned at the beginning of this chapter, we all need older people in our lives who can offer us the wisdom and encouragement they've acquired simply by being a few years ahead of us, or who might be considered more mature because they have gained knowledge and insight through personal experience.

What people come to mind when you think of those who have made a difference in your life because they were willing to pass along what they already know? List categories (pastors, teachers, relatives) or specific influencers by name.

_____

_____

_____

_____

_____

Have you ever been this person to others? If not, have you shied away from opportunity or do you think you just haven't recognized it as such?

_____

_____

_____

_____

_____

A little bit later in the chapter, you'll notice me becoming judgmental and cynical as my workload increased, as people didn't measure up to my ideals, and as I became more acquainted with my church's inner workings.

In what ways has judgmentalism crept into your own life?

_____

_____

_____

_____

_____

How can you intentionally check your own perspective in the moments you become disillusioned with your Christian brothers and sisters? In what ways can you combat a cynical mind-set?

_____

_____

_____

_____

_____

RESOLVE

Go to your favorite nursery or gardening supply store and buy a small sapling (or, check in with your local county extension agent who could help you find free or inexpensive trees). Plant the tree in a large container or visible location in your yard where you'll notice it often. Let it serve as a reminder to let your love for God and others flourish and grow, and to be careful not to let a "beam of wood" blind you to your own sins. If you're currently in a Titus 2–type relationship or would like to begin one (whether that means seeking someone to mentor you or intentionally mentoring someone else), invite someone to go tree shopping with you, and explain what you're doing and why you're doing it. It might be the beginning of a wonderful conversation . . . and friendship!

PRAY

Father God, thank You when You bring people into my life at just the right time to encourage me and point me to You right when I need it. Would You give me the skills and confidence to do the same for others? Lord, I confess that too often I'm quick to judge people You call me to love, or to impose my standards and expectations on them—expectations that have nothing to do with You. I am so grateful for the forgiveness You offer over and over again. Please reveal the areas in my life that have led me to wander and take my eyes off You. Thank You for the church, Your bride, and help me to glorify You by treating her well. In Your precious name, Amen.

12

SURPRISE PARTY

READ

I know, Lord, that a person's way of life is not his own; no one who walks determines his own steps. (Jer. 10:23)

Trust in the Lord with all your heart, and do not rely on your own understanding; in all your ways know him, and he will make your paths straight. (Prov. 3:5–6)

REFLECT

While we certainly have seasons of rest and calm, God has a way of moving in our lives—and asking us to move with Him. That may not always mean a physical move; it could mean a shift in our thinking or an attitude adjustment. Think about the last time God brought major change into your life.

Was it a move to a new place or something entirely different? Was it sudden or had it been sneaking up on you for a while? How did you handle the news and transition?

_____

_____

_____

_____

_____

What lessons did you learn in that season of change that you will bring with you in the next?

_____

_____

_____

_____

_____

Have you noticed anything different in your world lately? Is the "water heating up?" How so? Are you holding your current circumstances with a tight fist or open hand?

_____

_____

_____

_____

_____

Where can you see God's fingerprints in the changes you've experienced? Is it possible He's moving pieces around the board to make room for your next move? What do you think He's preparing you for?

_____

_____

_____

_____

_____

RESOLVE

Sometimes God calls us to make bold changes and sudden moves. Other times, though, He lets us warm up to the idea, and even encourages us by making our current state increasingly uncomfortable. Like the frog who acts differently in boiling water versus lukewarm water, our response to Him varies in those different scenarios. Next time you boil water for a cup of tea or pot of pasta, ask God if He's preparing you for a new season. Ask Him to open your eyes to "water" around you that might be dangerous or unhealthy. Ask Him to give you the courage and the faith to jump when He says jump.

PRAY

Father, thank You for the way You order our lives, and for the surprises that take us from one place to the next, whether literally or figuratively. Help me to receive each with equal grace. Teach me what it means to trust You with all my heart instead of my own understanding, and to know You so well I recognize the path You've planned for me rather than needlessly wandering. Help me move when You say to move. Thank You for the people You send into my life both to love and challenge me, and help me to be a better friend to all. Amen.

13

THE MAGIC OF STARTING OVER

READ

This is what the LORD says—who makes a way in the sea, and a path through raging water. . . . "Do not remember the past events, pay no attention to things of old. Look, I am about to do something new; even now it is coming. Do you not see it? Indeed, I will make a way in the wilderness, rivers in the desert." (Isa. 43:16, 18–19)

REFLECT

Think about the "happy places" in your own life.

What places (communities, groups of friends, physical locations) has God placed in your life as blessings? Have you thanked God for not only creating those places for you but leading you to them?

_____

_____

_____

_____

_____

How have those happy places strengthened your relationship with God or with others?

_____

_____

_____

_____

_____

RESOLVE

Print out a map of your community and mark your happy places on the map. This could be your church, a beautiful park, or a friend's house. It could be the store where you can find everything or the hill where you happen to see frequent sunsets. It could be the gym or the coffee shop. Any place where God has met you and blessed you, mark on the map. Tuck your map in this book, your Bible, or in a place where you'll see it often. As you're reminded of your happy places, thank God for meeting you where you are.

Or, if you're having trouble identifying happy places, is it possible you're anchored to your past? You can't change a thing from your past, but right this minute you can take God at His word and trust that He wants to do something new in your life, whether it's helping you see His current provision, opening a door of new opportunity, or making clear a next step to take. If you need a happy place in your life right now, ask God for one, and watch Him move.

PRAY

Father, You are sovereign and wise, controlling and allowing circumstances in our lives to conform us to the image of Your Son. I praise You for all the ways You provide for me, and ask You to help me to notice all the happy places in my life so I won't take a single provision for granted. I know that You "give and take away," and I confess that too often I try to take control and do things in my own strength. Thank You for Your patience with me, and for working all things together for my good and Your glory. I praise You, that in Christ, I am a new creation, and I'm grateful for Your new mercies every day. Help me to trust in You alone and to enjoy the blessings You give me while also holding them loosely. Give me the places in this season that will help remind me of Your goodness. Amen.

14

BACK AND FORTH

READ

For those who live according to the flesh have their minds set on the things of the flesh, but those who live according to the Spirit have their minds set on the things of the Spirit. Now the mind-set of the flesh is death, but the mind-set of the Spirit is life and peace. The mind-set of the flesh is hostile to God because it does not submit to God's law. Indeed, it is unable to do so. Those who are in the flesh cannot please God. You, however, are not in the flesh, but in the Spirit, if indeed the Spirit of God lives in you. If anyone does not have the Spirit of Christ, he does not belong to him. (Rom. 8:5–9)

REFLECT

The age-old battle of the flesh and spirit can manifest itself in so many ways. Take an honest look at yourself and think about how this battle shows up in your own life.

Do you tend to categorize sin in some type of hierarchy, rationalizing "minor" sins like jealousy, envy, strife, or selfish ambitions as not so bad?

_____

_____

_____

_____

_____

As you read through this passage of Scripture, how does it address this way of thinking?

_____

_____

_____

_____

_____

What are the evidences you see in your heart and life when you're led by the Spirit?

_____

_____

_____

_____

_____

Have you ever sensed a flesh vs. Spirit battle within your church? Have you ever felt concerned about behavior or decisions among its leaders? How did you handle those feelings? Did you address them with the person(s) involved? Or did you hold onto them, unsure if what you felt was true? How did that situation turn out?

_____

_____

_____

_____

_____

RESOLVE

When you find yourself taking issue or finding fault with your church, ministry, or peer group, it can be difficult to know if your complaints are valid, or if your concerns seem worse than they actually are due to a difficult personal season you are facing. If you are in this situation, can I challenge you to neither gloss over your concerns nor dwell on perceived slights?

Instead, commit to praying for discernment, asking God to make it crystal clear if your observations are from the Spirit or your flesh. Ask Him to test what you've observed or felt, and what He would have you do about it. Set an alarm on your phone to remind you to pray daily if it helps—for a week, month, or however long God is leading you. When the alarm goes off, stop each time to take your concerns to God and listen to His response. He tells us in the book of James that if we desire wisdom, we only need to ask for it. So rather than fussing or doubting or worrying, simply ask. And when He answers, listen to Him. If

He reveals that your concerns are due to your flesh or lack of perspective, simply confess that and return to Him. If He reveals that your concerns are valid, trust Him with this, and use your voice to start a loving discussion with the appropriate people.

PRAY

Father God, thank You for calling me to freedom. Please help me to use that freedom to serve others in love, not as an opportunity for my flesh to take over. Help me to walk by Your Spirit so I won't carry out the desires of my flesh. Change the way I think and behave so that my life produces fruit and bears testimony to Your transforming work in my heart. Give me confidence in my convictions and the discernment to follow Your leading to reach out to my sisters and brothers in the faith to address valid concerns when they come up. Thank You for giving me a mind to think and a voice to speak, and help me to steward them well and for Your glory. Amen.

15

ONCE UPON A BLOG

READ

"Do not have other gods besides me." (Exod. 20:3)

"Love the LORD your God with all your heart, with all your soul, and with all your strength." (Deut. 6:5)

"Don't store up for yourselves treasure on earth, where moth and rust destroy and where thieves break in and steal. But store up for yourselves treasures in heaven, where neither moth nor rust destroys, and where thieves don't break in and steal. For where your treasure is, there your heart will be also." (Matt. 6:19–21)

"For what does it benefit someone to gain the whole world and yet lose his life?" (Mark 8:36)

REFLECT

Throughout Scripture we are cautioned against placing our trust and hope in anything other than God. We are urged to worship Him first and foremost, to set clear boundaries, and to follow healthy, holy priorities. God knew how hard this would be for us, how challenging we would find consistent obedience, how easy it would be to stray. A good measure of our hearts is to examine our planner and our checkbook.

What do you learn about your priorities when you evaluate how you're spending your time, talents, resources, and money?

_____

_____

_____

_____

_____

What is your mind consumed with throughout the day? Is there one thing that demands the majority of your attention? Certainly, exceptions and context matter, and a simple metric like this doesn't tell the full story, so how else might you determine if you've allowed idols to creep into your life?

_____

_____

_____

_____

_____

How does your life look differently when you are most focused on Christ, in contrast to when your attention is either divided or even aimed completely toward something else?

_____

_____

_____

_____

_____

Do you have any safeguards in place to prevent yourself from leaning too much on things other than the Lord? What keeps your priorities firm and your heart true?

_____

_____

_____

_____

_____

RESOLVE

Listen to your favorite worship song or hymn that focuses on Jesus being the first or the center of our lives. If you don't know of one or would like to learn more songs that focus on this, ask a friend for a recommendation. Read the lyrics, soak up the truth, and use the music to point you back to Christ. Jesus is our greatest hope, and as such, He should be the center of our lives. Add songs that reminds you of those facts to your favorite playlist, or bookmark them in your browser. Listen often to remember that no person, no project, no ministry, and no mission should ever replace Jesus in our hearts or our lives.

PRAY

Father God, You alone are worthy of my worship, affections, and praise—perfect in all of Your ways. There is none like You, and I beg Your forgiveness when I place anything in my life before You. God, I want to love You with all my heart, soul, and strength, and to pursue eternal treasures and not the things of this world. I know this is not something I can do in my own strength, but only through the power of the Holy Spirit in me. Identify the things in my life I have put first, and help me turn from them and back to You. Show me all the ways You are a better place for me to find my worth, identity, and value. Help me to love You first and best, always. Amen.

16

EMPTY

READ

. . . give recognition to those who labor among you and lead you in the Lord and admonish you, and to regard them very highly in love because of their work. Be at peace among yourselves. And we exhort you, brothers and sisters: warn those who are idle, comfort the discouraged, help the weak, be patient with everyone. See to it that no one repays evil for evil to anyone, but always pursue what is good for one another and for all. Rejoice always, pray constantly, give thanks in everything; for this is God's will for you in Christ Jesus. (1 Thess. 5:12b–18)

REFLECT

Think of your own seasons of struggle or wandering, and the bumps in the road where church was difficult for you.

In your church experience, have you gone through a season of significant change or trials in a congregation? Perhaps a building campaign, staff turnover, member conflicts, or even (though, hopefully not) some sort of scandal?

_____

_____

_____

_____

How did the difficulties or challenges affect you and your faith journey?

_____

_____

_____

_____

_____

Did you question what happened or have concerns about the direction the church was going? How did you handle those questions or concerns—were you steadfast and resolved, or did you find yourself spiritually disoriented or disillusioned?

_____

_____

_____

_____

_____

Who did you turn to for help or solace during that time? Yourself? God? Trusted friends? Or did you keep the struggle buried in your heart?

How was the situation resolved, and what kind of lasting impact did that resolution have on your faith? We're called to submit to our spiritual authorities, but if you're in a season where you're struggling with this, you *can* follow God's will for your life according to the passage above: "rejoice always, pray constantly, and give thanks in everything."

RESOLVE

Commit to praying for the leaders of your church on a regular, on-going basis. Pray for their protection from temptation and discouragement and that their motives would be pure and above reproach. Pray for them to have increasing wisdom and discernment, to be fair, to be reasonable, to be without partiality, and to strive for unity and peace. Pray for their health, stamina, and energy, for their marriages and families, and for a flourishing relationship with the Lord. If you need help remembering to do this, create a reminder in your calendar or phone.

PRAY

Father God, thank You for every one of my church leaders, for all the workers and staff who serve You by loving our church body. Give them wisdom and discernment, and protect them from the evil one. Help them to love You first and most. Guard my heart from becoming judgmental and critical when I don't understand or agree with their decisions, but also give me the wisdom, insight, and courage to address valid concerns. Help all of us to be compassionate peacemakers and truth seekers. Break our hearts for what breaks Yours and keep us from advancing any sort of selfish agenda. Fill us with Your Spirit and empty us of ourselves. When my life is crumbling, all praise to You for being my firm foundation and precious cornerstone. Amen.

17

TUMBLING

READ

Now this is what the LORD says . . . "Do not fear, for I have redeemed you; I have called you by your name; you are mine. I will be with you when you pass through the waters, and when you pass through the rivers, they will not overwhelm you. You will not be scorched when you walk through the fire, and the flame will not burn you. For I am the LORD your God, the Holy One of Israel, and your Savior." (Isa. 43:1–3a)

REFLECT

Think of a time you've faced a crisis in your life.

What kind of challenges were you facing in this crisis—were they large and obvious or ordinary and subtle? Be specific.

_____

_____

_____

_____

_____

Did you try to exaggerate the positives and minimize the negatives instead of confronting and dealing with the deeper issues? How so?

_____

_____

_____

_____

_____

What are your go-to "idols," the things you are chasing like the wind to fill a void or add meaning to your life?

_____

_____

_____

_____

How do you react when you don't feel known and loved by the people closest to you, by friends, or even by work colleagues or acquaintances?

_____

_____

_____

_____

_____

What have you reached for instead of God in the seasons when you're grappling with your faith?

_____

_____

_____

_____

_____

RESOLVE

Make a written list of all the things you're struggling with, big or small. Get them down in black and white so you can see the full scope of this season you're in. Likewise, at the top of a separate page, record your primary love language (Gary Chapman, *The Five Love Languages*) and jot down all the ways you express love to others. Be specific.

Then, try to identify the love languages of those closest to you (dear friends, parents, spouse/significant other, children), how they express love, and how this differs from you. For even more insight, note how God loves you through all of these languages (you'll be surprised once you get creative with your answers).

When you're done with these written exercises, read back through this passage in Isaiah and consider how God is protecting, carrying, loving, and redeeming you in the midst of your "overwhelming waters" and "fiery flames." How are you actually being loved by God and others in ways that you might have previously missed? Thank Him for the ways He is working in your difficulties, challenges, sorrows, or voids. Because nothing happens apart from His plans or purposes, you can trust that He is not surprised by your circumstances, and He can use them for your good and His glory. Praise Him for calling you by name, considering you His own, filling your voids when you go to Him, and meeting you in crisis.

PRAY

Father God, thank You for the way You're working in my life, even in the midst of circumstances I wouldn't choose or don't understand. I confess that too often I look to things in this world to fill me when You are my greatest need. Thank You for receiving me as an honest beggar when I'm struggling with doubt or unbelief. Thank You for calling me yours when I'm chasing the wind and wavering in my faith. Thank You for opportunities disguised as heartache, and heartache disguised as opportunity, and for the way both reveal something of You. Thank You for promising You're always with me even when I'm oblivious to Your presence, and for being a better filler of my voids than anything else in this world. Amen.

18

THE PRECIPICE AND THE PIT

READ

I increased my achievements. . . . So I became great and surpassed all who were before me in Jerusalem; my wisdom also remained with me. All that my eyes desired, I did not deny them. I did not refuse myself any pleasure, for I took pleasure in all my struggles. This was my reward for all my struggles. *When I considered all that I had accomplished and what I had labored to achieve, I found everything to be futile and a pursuit of the wind. There was nothing to be gained under the sun.* (Eccles. 2:4a, 9–11, emphasis added)

When my soul was embittered, when I was pricked in heart, I was brutish and ignorant; I was like a beast toward you. Nevertheless, I am continually with you; you hold my right hand. You guide me with your counsel, and afterward you will receive me to glory. Whom have I in heaven but you? And there is nothing on earth that I desire besides you. My flesh and my heart may fail, but God is the strength of my heart and my portion forever. (Ps. 73:21–26 ESV)

REFLECT

Think about a lofty goal you've fixated on, expending considerable time, energy, money, and attention in order to achieve it.

Did it fill you in all the ways you anticipated or did it fall short? Explain.

_____

_____

_____

In what ways did pursuing this goal feel like you were chasing after the wind?

_____

_____

_____

Have you ever come face to face with what you consider to be the worst version of yourself? What were the circumstances pulling back the curtain, giving you a glimpse of this "monster"? How did you respond? Did you run toward God for help or away from Him in shame? Why?

_____

_____

_____

Do you recognize spiritual warfare when it's going on? When you remember that you have an enemy whose goal is to defeat you and the plans God has for your life, how does the realization change your mentality?

_____

_____

_____

How do you fight the enemy? Is this method working?

_____

_____

_____

In light of eternity, what is your greatest goal?

_____

_____

_____

RESOLVE

The next time you see a dandelion (or better yet, go outside and find one right now) pick it, make a wish, and blow it. As the seeds scatter in the breeze, think about the futility of our wishful thinking and endless efforts in light of God's values and economy. Ask God to reveal the ways you've become "the monster" who strives after the wrong things, and run to Him for transformation. Ask Him to replace your worldly desires with eternal values, and trust that He can transform monsters into beautiful creations. Let this ordinary weed serve as a two-fold reminder of the lessons Solomon teaches in the book of Ecclesiastes: one, to see and enjoy the gifts God lavishes on us, and two, to fear Him and keep His commands (Eccles. 12:13), which we do by "living each day with a humble awareness of our dependence on Him."[2]

PRAY

Father God, Your faithfulness amazes me, that You are always and only for me, even when I find myself in a season that I feel like a monster before You. There is nothing I've done to deserve the mercy and grace You've given me apart from Jesus alone. Thank You for giving me spiritual tools to fight spiritual battles and help me to remember to use them, to never forget who my real enemy is. I cannot believe how many times and in how many ways I blow it by trying to do things in my own strength. Thank You for letting me come to the end of myself if that's what it takes to recognize You as my only hope. Teach me to be dependent on You rather than proud of my independent and self-reliant ways. Show me the places where I'm chasing after the wind instead of chasing You. Thank You for Your outrageous love, the good gifts you give us to enjoy in this world, and for carrying me when I haven't even known You were there. May Your Spirit empower me to obey Your commands as I continue learning what it means to fear You, so that the days I wander would be increasingly seldom. Thank You for the gospel—which makes new creations out of all of us. Amen.

19

SURVIVAL INSTINCT

READ

Calling the crowd along with his disciples, he said to them, "If anyone wants to follow after me, let him deny himself, take up his cross, and follow me. For whoever wants to save his life will lose it, but whoever loses his life because of me and the gospel will save it. For what does it benefit someone to gain the whole world and yet lose his life?" (Mark 8:34–36)

REFLECT

Recall the survival stories of Aron Ralston and Louis Zamperini from this chapter, as well as any others you've heard through the years.

What stands out to you about the lengths people go to survive? Perhaps it's the pain they're willing to endure, their motivation to keep trying despite the odds, their positive attitude, tenacity, or something else.

_____

_____

_____

_____

_____

How does your survival instinct come into play in your faith, or in other words, what provisions are you making for your flesh (Rom. 13:14)? What does it look like for you to daily "deny yourself, take up your cross daily, and follow Jesus," essentially putting to death your fallen human tendencies?

_____

_____

_____

_____

_____

In what specific ways does the enemy tempt you most to let the "old self" live another day?

_____

_____

_____

_____

_____

RESOLVE

Many of us already have some sort of cross jewelry—earrings, necklaces, or bracelets with this iconic symbol of Christian faith. We wear them without a thought about what it actually is: an instrument of death, *the* instrument of death for our Lord and Savior, Jesus Christ. This would be a rather morbid practice if that's where our story ended, but praise God, it doesn't! The cross brings *good* news. It is where heaven meets earth, where Jesus bears the consequence of our sin and makes full atonement, the path through which He conquers death. If we question how much Jesus loves us, the answer is revealed with His arms open wide on a horizontal beam when He declares, "This much." When you wear your cross, let it serve as a frequent reminder of the lengths to which God has pursued you, even laying down His own life and conquering the enemy, while also helping you to remember to pick up your own cross, die to flesh, and follow Him.

PRAY

Father God, I'm astonished by what You were willing to do on my behalf while I was a sinner clinging to life, and even when I'm wandering in a desert. Thank You for making a way and for inviting me into Your forever-family. Lord, reveal to me the ways the enemy tempts me to let the old self take another breath. Also help me see the ways I fight to let my flesh stay alive, and teach me what it means to "pick up my cross and follow You" in ordinary, daily ways. Help my life to become more of You and less of me. I really, really mean it, help me make it so. For Your glory I offer this prayer and my life. Amen.

20

HELD

READ

And Jesus asked his father, "How long has this been happening to him?" And he said, "From childhood. And it has often cast him into fire and into water, to destroy him. But if you can do anything, have compassion on us and help us." And Jesus said to him, "'If you can'! All things are possible for one who believes." Immediately the father of the child cried out and said, "I believe; help my unbelief!" (Mark 9:21–24 ESV)

REFLECT

Think through a season where it was especially hard to believe that not only was God for you, but even His existence was questionable.

What was this faith-debilitating doubt like for you? What aspect of your faith did you question?

_____

_____

_____

_____

_____

Did you feel like you could admit, out loud, that you were no longer sure you believed in God? Who (if anyone) did you tell? How did that person respond?

_____

_____

_____

_____

Did you ever consider your questions as something God was using to bring you closer to Him? Why or why not?

_____

_____

_____

_____

Were you afraid to tell God? Or did you take your doubt to Him? How did He respond?

_____

_____

_____

_____

_____

Once you gave voice to the state of your heart to someone else, even if it was quietly before the Lord, what happened next?

_____

_____

_____

_____

_____

How has God used hard seasons in your past for good? Explain how knowing this can change the way you look at current (or future) seasons of doubt.

_____

_____

_____

_____

_____

RESOLVE

If you are experiencing doubt right now, I want to challenge you the same way my husband challenged me. If your once-strong faith is waning or wandering, what are you doing about it? I challenge you to face God and tell Him exactly what you're feeling and thinking. Tell Him you doubt; tell Him you have questions but no answers. Tell Him about wanting to walk away; tell Him exactly what it will take for you to choose faith again. Say it out loud, and see what happens. Then find a length of ordinary twine long enough to tie around your wrist. Knot it securely. Wear it as long as you need a reminder that God's faithfulness is not dependent on your faithfulness, and He's holding onto you even when you're tempted to let go.

PRAY

Father God, I am so thankful Your faithfulness has zero to do with my own. Thank You for the ways You love me no matter what, and that You went to the cross to prove it in a tangible way. It amazes me that You could even be using my doubts and disillusionment to bring me closer to You! Thank You for giving me the freedom to be honest with You, even when it's hard to be honest with myself and those I love most. You're ridiculously amazing and I'm grateful for Your unending grace. Amen.

21

LIFELINES

READ

"Consider how the wildflowers grow: They don't labor or spin thread. Yet I tell you, not even Solomon in all his splendor was adorned like one of these. If that's how God clothes the grass, which is in the field today and is thrown into the furnace tomorrow, how much more will he do for you—you of little faith?" (Luke 12:27–28)

REFLECT

Think about the places you have experienced God recently.

Do you intentionally look for Him or are you surprised when He shows up? Jot down some of the ways He's revealed Himself to you.

_____

_____

_____

_____

Where do you most often find the Lord—in nature, in a Sunday morning sermon, listening to music or a podcast, in Scripture, in small, unexpected blessings, in protection you only learn about later, or something else altogether?

_____

_____

_____

_____

_____

If you look back on your life, can you identify any places where He was present and moving, though you didn't see Him working at the time?

_____

_____

_____

_____

_____

What are your personal "rainbow" stories—places in your life where you can confidently say, "I know that was God!"? How does that memory help you in this current season or when you're struggling?

_____

_____

_____

_____

_____

RESOLVE

Begin a journal specifically to record lifelines, God-winks, and miracles. Don't limit it to what happens for you alone; also include those times people tell you about miracles happening in their lives (perhaps even something *you've* said or done is an answer to prayer for them). Every time you realize something you experience is a gift from God, write it down. Record His fingerprints in your life and you'll have a treasure trove of memories to encourage you when life gets hard or you're tempted to question His presence and goodness toward you.

PRAY

Father God, I marvel at how You keep showing up in the world, in the beauty of nature, in the lives of those who follow You, and in Your holy Word. I'm realizing more and more that You tell us to seek You in Your Word because You want to be found, and also because we're so prone to forget to seek You in the first place. Thank You for answering the prayers of my heart in Your perfect way and according to Your will—in a sermon, in a letter, or even sometimes in a rainbow. Thank You for Your kindness in showing evidences of Yourself when we're looking and sometimes even when we fail to seek. Open my eyes and heart not only to see You, but to be eager to share what I have seen with others. When the world is dark, thank You for sending Light. Amen.

22

TORNADO

READ

I lift my eyes toward the mountains. Where will my help come from? My help comes from the LORD, the Maker of heaven and earth. He will not allow your foot to slip; your Protector will not slumber. Indeed, the Protector of Israel does not slumber or sleep. The LORD protects you; the LORD is a shelter right by your side. The sun will not strike you by day or the moon by night. The LORD will protect you from all harm; he will protect your life. The LORD will protect your coming and going both now and forever. (Ps. 121)

REFLECT

Recall a time in your life (or someone else's life, if not yours) when you faced a terrifying situation or even a near-death experience. What happened?

How did you feel in the middle of that experience—and what did you do?

_____

_____

_____

_____

_____

Did you call on the name of Jesus to save you? What does your response tell you about your faith at that time?

_____

_____

_____

_____

_____

Why do you think people reflexively call out to God in these types of situations? When push comes to shove, why do we naturally trust Him with the power of life and death?

_____

_____

_____

_____

_____

RESOLVE

Revisit the section in this chapter when the game *"What would we do if we were in their shoes?"* was discussed. Why not try the exercise yourself? Think of people in your life who have experienced tragedy, or who are currently in the midst of difficult circumstances right now. Put yourself in their shoes and try to imagine how you would want to respond if this actually happened to you. How would you cope, react, and interact with others who are affected? What does your imagined response reveal about your relationship with God? If you aren't satisfied with your gut response or instinct, take some time to think about why that is and what you'd like to do differently.

PRAY

Father God, You alone are mighty and able to save. Thank You for reminding me throughout Scripture that You are always with us in our day-to-day lives but also in the worst of storms. Your timing and Your provision isn't always what I expect, but I can trust that both are just what I need. May Your name always be on my lips, in the bad times, yes, but also in the good. Amen.

23

IT'S A WONDERFUL LIFE

READ

"Simon, Simon, look out. Satan has asked to sift you like wheat. *But I have prayed for you that your faith may not fail. And you, when you have turned back, strengthen your brothers.*" "Lord," he told him, "I'm ready to go with you both to prison and to death." "I tell you, Peter," he said, "the rooster will not crow today until you deny three times that you know me." (Luke 22:31–34, emphasis added).

REFLECT

The odds of your being born are incredibly slim. With this in mind:

Have you figured out what on earth you are here for? What are your long-held dreams? It's a hard question for many of us to answer, but it begins in trusting that God knows and loves you, and that He has a plan and purpose for your life. What are the things you might try if failure wasn't an option?

_____

_____

_____

Do you regard God's decision to give you life on this earth as an accident, as arbitrary, or as a purposeful, divine decision? How might your life look different if you genuinely believed God gave you this life for a reason?

_____

_____

_____

Think about the greatest difficulties you've faced for a moment, times when tragedy struck close to home or when you knowingly disobeyed God and had to suffer the consequences. Assuming you've moved beyond these things and found healing or forgiveness or victory, imagine that Jesus is saying to you what He said to Simon Peter in the passage above (personalizing it): _"I have prayed for you that your faith may not fail. Now, that you're on 'this' side of 'that,' use it to strengthen and encourage your sisters and brothers."_

_____

_____

_____

Are you able to see, now that you have some time, space, and hindsight, how God put all the puzzle pieces together for an incredible picture made richer and more beautiful _because_ of your personal experience? How so?

_____

_____

_____

How might you "give from your void" as mentioned in this chapter, sharing what you've learned and endured with others who are currently struggling?

_____

_____

_____

What blessing, counsel, or influence might be missing from others' lives if *you* weren't around to offer what only you are equipped and experienced to give?

_____

_____

_____

RESOLVE

Have a movie night! *Watch It's a Wonderful Life* (even if it's not Christmas time), *Back to the Future*, or *The Family Man*. Think about all the parts of your life that could have been altered if you had made different choices at specific junctures in your own life, but now wouldn't change for the world. Thank God for the way He's remained faithful to you through all your twists and turns, and ask Him what He has planned for you next.

PRAY

Father, thank You for giving me this gift of life, to make a difference for others, of course, but also to bear Your image in a broken and hurting world. It's overwhelming to know You are praying for my faith not to fail, and that my past hurts and even the consequences of poor or sinful decisions might be used to equip me to strengthen others. Help me to see that not even one moment of my wandering is wasted, and to recognize the hard and holy work You're accomplishing, always ready to give an account of what You're making new in my life. I'm humbled to think You are mindful of me, yet I know it's the work and wonder of Jesus living in and through me that matters now and for all of eternity. You alone are worthy of my praise. Amen.

24

ALWAYS REMEMBER

READ

"Listen, Israel: The LORD our God, the LORD is one. Love the LORD your God with all your heart, with all your soul, and with all your strength. These words that I am giving you today are to be in your heart. Repeat them to your children. Talk about them when you sit in your house and when you walk along the road, when you lie down and when you get up. Bind them as a sign on your hand and let them be a symbol on your forehead. Write them on the doorposts of your house and on your city gates." (Deut. 6:4–9)

REFLECT

As I suggested in this chapter, one of Satan's sharpest tools is inflicting memory loss. He wants you to forget Whose you are (belonging to God Almighty), and he wants you to forget who you are (a child of God and co-heir with Christ, wholly known and loved by the Lord). Wandering begins when you lose sight of either of those two things.

When you forget these things, how can you remind yourself to return to the kind of life that is governed by love and lived in obedience to God?

_____

_____

_____

_____

_____

Why do you think reminding yourself of these two things is so important? What's at stake?

_____

_____

_____

_____

_____

How does it make you feel to know the enemy of your heart delights in your Bible illiteracy? Since Satan doesn't want you to know what the Bible says, to understand and memorize Scripture, and to know who God is and who He says you are, what are you going to do about it?

_____

_____

_____

RESOLVE

Scripture memorization comes easier for some than others, but it is enlightening, heartening, important, and life-giving for all of us. Think about your current circumstances and choose four relevant verses to memorize over the next month, just one per week. Perhaps you need to be reminded of God's faithfulness (there are several listed in this chapter). Or maybe you're struggling with identity and need to hear who God says you are in contrast to the mixed messages culture and media are blasting. If so, you might want to refer back to the list on pages 206–207 and memorize some of the passages referenced there.

Psalm 119:11 says, "I have treasured your word in my heart so that I may not sin against you." Having God's word on our hearts steers us away from sinning against him—yet another reason to strengthen your resolve to follow through. Jot down your selected passages on sticky notes and adhere them to your bathroom mirror; write them on index cards and keep them in your bag to pull out and go over whenever you have a spare moment; or type them up, print them out, and use pens, markers, or paints to make a lovely piece of Scripture art. If you have a good space for it, consider writing the verses on the walls of your home! Wherever and however it will help you, find a way to commit these passages to memory.

PRAY

Father God, give me a hunger for Your Word to better know You, and to better understand beyond a shadow of a doubt who You tell me I am. Dull the lies of the world and silence the enemy's seductive whisper so that Yours is the only voice I hear. Help me always to remember that You are a God like none other, that You have all knowledge, ability, power, love, and royal authority over this world. Also, help me remember who I am in light of that: I am a daughter dearly loved by a King, fearfully and wonderfully made, and You know me and call me by name. Amen.

25

NOT ALL WHO WANDER ARE LOST

READ

Be gracious to me, God, for a man is trampling me; he fights and oppresses me all day long. My adversaries trample me all day, for many arrogantly fight against me. When I am afraid, I will trust in you. In God, whose word I praise, in God I trust; I will not be afraid. What can mere mortals do to me? They twist my words all day long; all their thoughts against me are evil. They stir up strife, they lurk; they watch my steps while they wait to take my life. Will they escape in spite of such sin? God, bring down the nations in wrath. *You yourself have recorded my wanderings. Put my tears in your bottle. Are they not in your book? Then my enemies will retreat on the day when I call. This I know: God is for me.* In God, whose word I praise, in the LORD, whose word I praise, in God I trust; I will not be afraid. What can mere humans do to me? I am obligated by vows to you, God; I will make my thank offerings to you. For you rescued me from death, even my feet from stumbling, to walk before God in the light of life. (Ps. 56, emphasis added)

REFLECT

Think about this current season of your life, and reflect in this final chapter.

Where are you today, friend? Are you wandering in the desert? Questioning your faith or even God Himself? Or if this isn't the case for you and you've been reading along with someone else in mind, record your reasons for concern.

_____

_____

_____

_____

_____

Can you see the solid ground from here, a place set apart on the other side of all this struggle, where you are strong in the Lord? Do you feel afraid you'll never get there? If so, take some time to write out how you're feeling right now.

_____

_____

_____

_____

_____

Or have you already crossed over, relieved to be enjoying a newfound, fiery faith in the Lord, though perhaps a little weary from your travels? If this is where you are, stop to thank God for such a vibrant season of faith, a gift straight from His hand.

_____

_____

_____

_____

_____

Wherever you are, God is already there. Whether you feel lost or found or somewhere in between, God knows exactly where you are and He will be faithful to you every step of the way. God is always and only for you. He will not abandon you, no matter how long you struggle and question and wonder and wander. He will not let you go, and He will not let any of your journey go to waste.

RESOLVE

Right now, pull out your journal, a planner, or the calendar on your phone (wherever you record important dates). Write a note to commemorate this day; if it's on your phone, make it pop up as an annual reminder. No matter where you are on your spiritual journey, no matter how many unanswered questions you still hold or how many scars you might bear, do something to help you remember this exact moment: the time you realized or remembered that just because you're wondering doesn't mean you're lost, and that you are still secure in God's grip.

Then, if you don't already have some among your kitchen spices, buy a jar of mustard seeds. Read from the Gospel accounts where Jesus talks about faith relative to the size of this little seed (Matt. 13 and 17; Luke 17; Mark 4). Carefully extract one seed and notice how tiny it is in your hand. Imagine that it represents the size of your faith, and remember what Jesus says—that even a small amount can accomplish big things. You may want to keep a small vial or decorative container of mustard seeds in your kitchen window or a similar visible location where you can continually be reminded of God's limitless power in contrast to your small but honest faith.

PRAY

Father God, help me to bring glory to You by finding my greatest satisfaction in You. Please continue Your transforming work in my life that I might "also consider everything to be a loss in view of the surpassing value of knowing Christ Jesus my Lord" (Phil. 3:8a). Make my goal be to know You and make You known, to love You and others because of Your great love for me. Thank You that even when the only prayer I can offer is, "I believe. Help my unbelief," Your love and grace never waver. Praise You, indeed, for Your unfailing faithfulness, for making mine a redemption story, and that all who wander are not actually lost. Amen.

NOTES

1. This translation of Dante's *The Divine Comedy: The Inferno, Purgatorio, and Paradiso* comes from the Everyman's Library Series, translated by Allen Mandelbaum and introduced by Peter Armour (New York: Knopf Doubleday Publishing Group, 1995).

2. From the introduction to Ecclesiastes in *(in)courage Devotional Bible* (Nashville, TN: Holman Bible Publishers, 2018), 905.

LET'S CONNECT!

A former marketing and PR professional, Robin Dance now encourages others in life and faith as a writer, speaker, and small group leader. She believes listening well, laughter, and generosity are indispensable superpowers, and there might not be a sweeter ministry than a gift of home-baked bread. Robin advocated for children in poverty as a Compassion International blogger in Kolkata, and she has been a regular contributor to (in)courage, DaySpring's online community for women, since its inception. Married to her college sweetheart and mom to a daughter and two sons, Robin is a fan of good stories, and her favorite is the one you're dying to share.

 robindance.me    robindance.me

facebook.com/RobinBDance   robindance

 Robin@robindance.me   #ForAllWhoWanderBook

(in)courage
welcomes you

to a place where authentic, brave women
connect deeply with God and others.
Through the power of shared stories and
meaningful resources, (in)courage champions
women and celebrates the strength Jesus gives
to live out our calling as God's daughters.
In the middle of your unfine moments and ordinary days,
you are invited to become a woman of courage.

Join us at **www.incourage.me** and
connect with us on social media!

@incourage

The **CSB (in)courage Devotional Bible** invites every woman to find her story *within the* greatest story ever told—God's story *of* redemption.

- **312 devotions** by 122 (in)courage community writers

- 10 distinct thematic **reading plans**

- Stories of courage from **50 women** of the Bible

- *and more features!*

Find out more at **incourageBible.com**

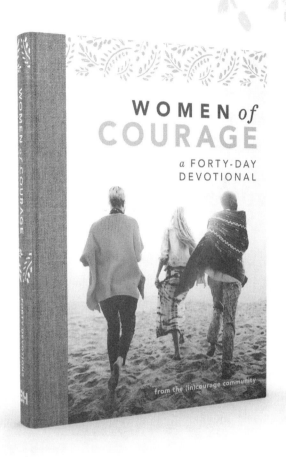

You are a Woman *of* Courage...
Because God says so.

Featuring 40 brave women from the Bible, this devotional will walk with you through the hardest days and leave you with the courage you need to lead, to love, to trust, and to turn to God in every situation.

Available now wherever books are sold.